Lynton and Lynmouth

Situated where the western fringes of Exmoor slope down to the sea and backed by thickly wooded hills, **Lynmouth** is a delightful resort. Here the river mouth forms a tiny harbour (*below*), sheltered by a stone jetty. Among the picturesque cottages on Mars Hill (*left*), which overlooks the harbour, is the Rising Sun Hotel, which dates from the 14th century and was once used by smugglers. Next to it stands Shelley's cottage where the poet lived after his elopement with his 16-year-old bride.

Situated high above Lynmouth, **Lynton** (*right*) clings to the slopes of the hill where it is perched some 500 feet above the sea in the midst of the dramatic scenery of this heritage coast. From the top of Countisbury Hill there are superb views over the Bristol Channel with Lynton and Lynmouth clearly visible between the hills. Lynton became popular with visitors in Victorian and Edwardian times and much of its architecture reflects this period.

Linking cliff-top Lynton with Lynmouth below is the spectacular Cliff Railway (*left*) which opened in 1890. The 862 feet long track climbs about 500 feet and the lift operates on a system of counter-balance. Each passenger car has a 700 gallon ballast tank which is filled with water at the top and emptied at the bottom so that as the heavier car descends, it automatically raises the empty one to the top again.

Near Lynton, the East Lyn River and the Hoaroak Water come together at **Watersmeet** (*right*) where the water cascades over the boulder-strewn river bed. There are many beautiful walks through the wooded valley where the scenery is a delight in all seasons. West of Lynton is the dramatic **Valley of Rocks** (*below*). The poet Southey described these jagged granite pinnacles as "rock reeling upon rock, stone piled upon stone, a huge terrific mass". The great bulk of Castle Rock is one of the highest sea cliffs in Britain, dropping 800 feet to the shore.

Exmoor

Exmoor has a fascinating variety of scenery, much of which is best explored on foot or on horseback. It offers a rich habitat for wildlife including an occasional otter and many types of birds from the mighty buzzard to the tiny nuthatch. Red deer roam wild on the moor together with the typical small-horned sheep and the famous Exmoor ponies. These sturdy, rough-coated animals move freely over the moors in all weathers, but are somewhat timid and difficult to approach. In the heart of the moor is **Landacre Bridge** (*below*), a fine five-arched medieval bridge which spans the River Barle with one foot in Devon and the other in Somerset.

The lovely River Barle, noted for its excellent salmon and trout fishing, is one of the principal rivers of Exmoor. Near Dulverton it is spanned by **Tarr Steps** (*above*), an impressive 180 feet long causeway which is the longest clapper bridge in Britain. It was probably constructed in pre-historic times and consists of vast stone slabs, some of which weigh as much as five tons, laid on uprights in the bed of the stream. Offering superb views in all directions, **Dunkery Beacon** is the highest point in Somerset at 1,705 feet, and is crowned with a large stone cairn (*below right*) which commemorates the acquisition of the area by The National Trust in 1934. The **Fortescue Cairn** (*below left*) was erected in memory of Sir John Fortescue, 1859-1933, librarian at Windsor Castle, and a keen walker and naturalist who also wrote books about this area. Situated at Blue Gate near Simonsbath, it overlooks the wild expanse of Exmoor towards Drybridge Combe.

A patchwork of fertile meadowlands separates the graceful sweep of **Porlock Bay** (*above*), site of a Danish landing in 886 AD, from the village of **Porlock** which is sheltered on three sides by the uplands of the Exmoor National Park. Now left inland by the retreating sea, this one-time port has a narrow, winding main street which is lined with the ancient thatch-roofed cottages which are typical of West Country architecture and particularly abundant in this area. The picturesque Ship Inn (*centre*), parts of which date back to the 13th century, is a well-known landmark. The poet Robert Southey was a frequent visitor and a chimney-corner in the inn is dedicated to him. The picturesque little seaside village of **Porlock Weir** (*below*) lies at the western end of Porlock Bay. The tiny harbour, overlooked by colour-washed cottages and old inns, was once busy with coasters carrying timber to South Wales in exchange for coal. It is still a popular port of call, although today it is used mainly by pleasure craft.

West Somerset contains numerous beautiful stone-built villages where many of the farmhouses and cottages date from the 16th to the 18th centuries. The delightful village of **Bossington** (*right*) lies at the seaward end of the Vale of Porlock, sheltered beneath 800 feet high Bossington Hill. This lovely old thatched cottage with its round chimneys is typical of many found in this area. Situated on the northern edge of Exmoor, picturesque **Allerford** (*centre*) is an ancient village recorded in the Domesday Book. A centre for some fine woodland walks, it has an unusual thatched school house and a number of quaint cottages built of local red sandstone. Paved with cobbles, the attractive, double-arched medieval pack-horse bridge enabled mules, donkeys and horses to carry their loads of wool across the River Aller.

Situated between Minehead and Porlock, the charming village of **Selworthy** (*left*) clings to wooded slopes beneath 1,014 feet high Selworthy Beacon. Looking out across the lush valley to Dunkery and the Exmoor hills, the village is known for its numerous fine thatched cottages, 14th century church and ancient tithe barn. Along with much of the surrounding countryside, the village is protected by The National Trust.

The ford which originally gave **Exford** (*above*) its name has long been replaced by a handsome stone bridge. Situated in the heart of Exmoor, this large village is noted for its traditional rural pursuits. A popular resort for fishing enthusiasts, it is also the setting for a famous annual Horse Show. Standing beneath Dunkery Beacon, secluded **Luccombe** (*centre*) is but one of a number of pretty little villages which reflect the rural traditions of West Somerset. Many of the picturesque cottages date from medieval times and were refurbished in the early 19th century to house estate workers. The church, which dates from the 13th century, has a barrel-roof with

carved bosses and contains the tomb of a previous rector who raised a Royalist troop during the Civil War in which four of his sons were captains. **Withypool** (*bottom*) was once the chief village on the moor. Today it is a quiet, unspoiled village and a favourite haunt of anglers. On Withypool Common can be seen the remains of an ancient stone circle.

Exmoor villages are close and compact, each with its complement of ancient cottages and charming old inns. **Winsford** (*above*), birthplace in 1881 of the statesman Ernest Bevin, stands in a wooded valley on the eastern edge of Exmoor. Overlooking one of several ancient pack-horse bridges which span the River Winn nearby, the handsome Royal Oak Inn was originally a farmhouse and dairy. It developed into a hostelry to meet the needs of the growing pack-horse cart traffic which came with the growth of the wool trade.

Beautifully situated on the southern fringes of the moor, **Dulverton** (*left*) is a charming country town which makes an ideal centre for exploring the varied scenery of Exmoor. The Church of All Saints was much restored in Victorian times but it retains a 12th century tower. The Lorna Doone Statue (*above*) stands in the main square outside the Exmoor National Park Centre which houses exhibitions about the heritage of Dulverton and the surrounding area.

Dunster and Minehead

The little market town of **Dunster** is dominated by its hill-top castle which was the home of the Luttrell family for 600 years. Originally built in 1070 it was remodelled several times over the following centuries and is now owned by The National Trust. Picturesque Rose Cottage (*below*) is typical of the many attractive thatch-roofed, colour-washed cottages which enrich the countryside in this part of Somerset.

Among the other interesting old buildings in Dunster is a 17th century water-mill, a beautiful old building of mellow brick, stone and plaster, and a tiny Benedictine priory which flourished from Norman times until the 1530s when Henry VIII dissolved the monasteries. A substantial number of the original monastic buildings remain including a tithe barn, a 13th century dovecote, the monks' lodging, now a private house, and the priory church. The delightful monks' garden has been converted into a Garden of Remembrance, honouring those who gave their lives in two world wars. The distinctive eight-sided Yarn Market stands in the main street and dates from the time when the town was an important wool market and weaving centre. Dunster's fine church (*left*) was originally built in the 12th century and was once used both as the parish church and by the monks of the nearby priory. It contains a remarkable carved rood screen, one of the longest in the world at fifty-four feet. It was built to separate the monks of the priory from the parishioners.

An attractive modern resort with a mile-long seafront, splendid sands and a mild climate, **Minehead** is a popular centre for touring Exmoor and the Somerset coast. Formerly it was an important port, trading with Africa and North America, but the harbour began to silt up in the late 18th century and it now offers a small but attractive haven for fishermen and pleasure boats. Composed of delightful, irregularly built cottages, Church Town (*top*) is the old part of Minehead, clustered around the 15th century parish church. Minehead Station (*right*) is the western terminus of the West Somerset Railway, Britain's longest preserved railway. It runs for twenty miles through superb countryside along the coast from Minehead to Dunster, Blue Anchor and Watchet where it turns inland to Bishop's Lydeard.

Lorna Doone Country

The north-western part of Exmoor, between Lynton and Porlock, has become closely associated with the **Doone Country,** so vividly portrayed by R. D. Blackmore in his romantic novel *Lorna Doone*. When John Ridd discovered the Doone Valley (*left*), he had been poaching by the Badgworthy water, and the valley is thought to lie near the waterslide at Lank Combe. Blackmore probably combined elements from Badgworth, Hoccombe and Lank Combe to create the valley of the notorious Doones.

In all probability, the original farmstead called "Plover's Barrows" in the story no longer exists but this fine farmhouse at **Malmsmead** (*above*) has come to be known as Lorna Doone Farm. Near it an ancient ford crosses picturesque Badgworthy Water. Gateway to Doone Country, **Brendon** is one of Exmoor's showpiece villages. The lovely old Church of St. Brendon (*right*) retains two fine Norman fonts.

The Exmoor hamlet of **Oare** is at the heart of the Lorna Doone country, for it was on the altar steps of tiny St. Mary's Church at Oare (*above*) that Lorna was shot by Carver Doone during her marriage to John Ridd. At the time of the story the church, which dates from the 14th and 15th centuries, would only have held about twelve people. The chancel was enlarged in the mid-19th century, by which time box pews had been added. There are several interesting old items in the church which also contains a portrait of R. D. Blackmore which was erected in 1925 as a memorial to the author on the centenary of his birth. Three of Exmoor's delightful streams, Oare Water, Chalk Water and Weir Water, come together near the tiny hamlet of Oareford. Here stands **Robber's Bridge** (*left*), surrounded by some of the most remote parts of the moor. It is said to be the bridge over which the notorious Doones rode on their way back to Doone Valley.

Ilfracombe and Combe Martin

Lying in a deep sheltered combe or valley, **Combe Martin** (*right* and *bottom*) is a popular resort best known for its coves and fine coastal walks. The beach is flanked by rocks which form a secluded harbour where small boats shelter. With its majestic cliffs and rocky headlands, picturesque bays and secluded beaches, this is one of the most memorable stretches of coast in England. Nearby **Berrynarbor** (*right*) is a charming village with a fine part-Norman church and a number of quaint old cottages at its heart. Perched between coast and combe, it is both a holiday centre and an agricultural community with several farms lying behind the village above the valley slopes.

The long, narrow inlet at **Watermouth Cove** (*above*) provides a sheltered haven for small boats of all kinds. It is situated to the east of Ilfracombe on an impressive stretch of coast where the jagged cliffs and rocky coves are washed by the Bristol Channel. The cove is overlooked by neo-Gothic Watermouth Castle which was built in 1825 and now houses a museum including relics of the days of smuggling. The delightful little sandy coves at **Woody Bay** and **Lee Bay** (*below*) nestle at the foot of the cliffs between Combe Martin and Lynton. Woody Bay takes its name from the oak woods which sweep right down to the sea. Lee Bay, also sheltered by high tree-clad slopes, is one of the more accessible beaches on this stretch of coast. There are splendid coastal views from the top of the cliffs which also provide a breeding site for many varieties of sea-bird including auks, guillemots, kittiwakes, fulmars, shags and razorbills.

Built in terraces on the steep hills which rise up from the shore, **Ilfracombe** was developed during Victorian times and is now North Devon's largest holiday resort. Surrounded on three sides by attractive colour-washed buildings, the harbour has for centuries offered a refuge for seafarers on this rugged stretch of coast and today it is still busy with fishing boats and pleasure craft. Beatrix Potter, author of many famous nursery classics, spent childhood holidays in Ilfracombe and in *The Tale of Little Pig Robinson*, she describes the "long flight of steps to the harbour basin".

There are magnificent views of the town from Hillsborough Hill, a headland which rises from the sea to a height of 447 feet. In the heart of the town are the colourful Runnymede Gardens (*right*), one of several attractive open spaces which enhance the resort's appeal to visitors and residents alike.

Pretty little Lee Bay is a sheltered cove which lies at the foot of a deep, wooded valley to the west of Ilfracombe. Here fuchsias and hydrangeas grow in such profusion that it is often known as "Fuchsia Valley". **Lee Village** stands on the North Devon Coast Path behind the bay. Among the interesting old buildings in the village is the thatched cottage of the "Old Maids of Lee" (*right*) which is believed to date from 1653. The Three Old Maids

appeared in a Victorian song and are said to have lived here at one time. The gardens at **Arlington Court** (*below*), now owned by The National Trust, combine a formal, terraced Victorian garden with largely informal areas where spring bulbs and wild flowers carpet the grass. The herbaceous borders, rockery and conservatory make a pleasing contrast with the wilderness area where rhododendrons and hydrangeas thrive in the acid soil and mild, damp climate.

Woolacombe and Croyde

In a sheltered curve between Morte Point and Baggy Point the golden sands of Woolacombe Bay sweep southwards for more than two miles creating some of the finest beaches in the West Country. Behind it the grassy, gorse-clad slopes of Woolacombe Down offer superb views across the Bristol Channel.

The westward-facing beach at **Woolacombe** (*top*) is popular with bathers and also ideal for surfing. At its northern end is the narrow inlet which is known as Barricane Beach (*above*). Framed by rocks and noted for its sea shells, the tiny cove is sometimes also called Shell Beach. Set on a steep hill above Woolacombe, in an area renowned for its outstanding natural beauty, **Mortehoe** (*right*) is a good centre for walkers. One of numerous rocky inlets along this part of the coast, it is sheltered by Morte Point, a treacherous reef which claimed many lives in the days of sail.

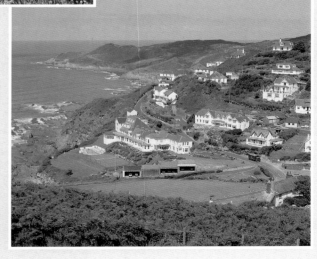

Situated in an area of North Devon which is famous for its impressive coastal scenery, the little village of **Croyde** (*above* and *right*) is full of old-world charm. Here there are several picturesque, colour-washed cottages with thatched roofs and attractive gardens which are a delight whatever the season. Together with nearby Croyde Bay, this picturesque little village attracts many visitors. **Croyde Bay** (*below*) is one of Devon's finest surfing beaches. It is crossed by little streams and sheltered to the north and south by grassy headlands. From Croyde Bay the Somerset and North Devon Coast Path takes walkers round the headland to Baggy Point from where there are magnificent views which take in Lundy Island some fifteen miles offshore.

Braunton (*above*), which claims to be the largest village in England, is a popular centre for visitors to North Devon. It has developed considerably in recent years but the oldest part, which is set on sloping hills, consists of a quaint mixture of narrow streets, cottages and old inns. The church, a building of great beauty and interest, is dedicated to St. Brannock, the 6th century Celtic saint from whom the village takes its name. **Saunton Sands** (*below*) is a three-mile-long expanse of sand which is one of Devon's finest holiday beaches. Facing due west, it provides ideal conditions for surfers.

The Taw and Torridge

An ancient seaport and shipbuilding town with a history which dates back to Saxon times, **Barnstaple** (*above*) is situated on the River Taw. The famous Long Bridge was first built for pack-horses in the late 13th century and retains much of the original medieval work. Barnstaple has always been known as a market town and the **Pannier Market** (*right*) dates from the 1850s. It acquired its name from the baskets, or panniers, in which produce was brought to market.

Marwood Hill Gardens (*left*) near Barnstaple contain more than 5,000 different varieties of plants in a splendid valley setting. A mature garden, but one that is constantly being augmented and updated, it is known for its magnificent flowering shrubs as well as plantings of willows, ferns and eucalyptus. The gardens also feature three small lakes, a bog garden and a glasshouse containing an exceptional collection of camellias.

South Molton and its smaller neighbour North Molton both lie in the valley of the River Mole, from which they take their name. **South Molton** (*top*) is an ancient market town which received borough status in 1301 and obtained a charter from Queen Elizabeth I. It retains some fine Georgian houses and the Guildhall, with its attractive arcaded lower storey, dates from 1743. The church at **North Molton** (*bottom*) has a fine medieval pulpit. Situated in a beautiful woodland setting with a stream and a trout lake, **Broomhill Sculpture Garden** (*centre*) has been developed over the last ten years on the site of gardens which had been neglected for many decades. Scattered around the ten-acre site are 300 works by sculptors of international renown, all superbly integrated with the natural environment, and reached by winding paths through the woods and around the lake.

Standing at the end of a long tree-lined drive, **Tapeley Park** (*above*) is an impressive 17th century mansion which is enhanced by a beautiful terraced Italian garden. Much altered and enlarged, the house retains some remarkable ceilings as well as fine porcelain and glass. It is spectacularly situated overlooking the Taw and Torridge estuary near Bideford. **Bideford** (*left* and *bottom*) was once a busy port with ships trading to North America and the West Indies, and the tree-lined quay is still well used by small coasters. An attractive market town, it is situated on the lovely River Torridge, spanned here by a splendid bridge of twenty-four arches.

Cobbled streets and colour-washed buildings add to the character of the ancient fishing village of **Appledore** (*left*) which is situated where the estuaries of the Rivers Taw and Torridge meet. The picturesque old quay where sailing ships once moored is still at the centre of local life and aspects of the town's long seafaring history are illustrated in a local maritime museum.

Picturesque **Instow** (*right*) is popular both with artists and holiday-makers. From bustling Instow Quay, headquarters of the North Devon Yacht Club, a ferry plies across the river to Appledore.

Although it is a relatively modern creation, **Westward Ho!** (*below*) has a number of literary associations. Founded in 1863, the village took its name from Charles Kingsley's famous novel about Elizabethan seafarers. Kipling's Tor, to the west of the village, is named after another author, Rudyard Kipling, who was a student at the United Services College here. Overlooking Bideford Bay, Westward Ho! boasts a fine three-mile expanse of sands which is backed by a remarkable ridge of pebbles.

The beautiful gardens at **Rosemoor** (*left*) are maintained by The Royal Horticultural Society. They comprise a number of themed areas including a stream and bog garden, an ornamental vegetable garden and a herb garden. In addition to the colourful herbaceous borders, Rosemoor has an extensive rose garden with more than 200 varieties of roses.

Great Torrington (*centre*) is an ancient town which was known as a market before the time of the Norman Conquest. The Market Square is surrounded by a number of interesting and attractive old buildings and at its centre there is an elaborately decorated fountain.

From its position on a hill, Great Torrington gives superb views across the countryside described in Henry Williamson's famous novel *Tarka the Otter*. The **Tarka Trail** (*left* and *below*), a 180-mile-long network of footpaths, follows the story of Tarka's travels across the two great national parks of Exmoor and Dartmoor, along a section of the coastal path and through the lovely Torridge Valley.

Clovelly and Hartland

Attracting visitors and artists from all over the world, the enchanting village of **Clovelly** clings to the cliffs overlooking Bideford Bay. The single street, known as Down-a-long or Up-a-long (*top*) depending on the direction travelled, descends steeply in steps past whitewashed cottages bright with flowers. The cobbled street is paved with pebbles from the beach and all cars are banned here. However, the famous Clovelly donkeys are still used to carry passengers and goods.

At the bottom of the hill, 400 feet below, is a tiny harbour (*bottom*) where the boats of the lobster fishermen tie up alongside pleasure craft at the 18th century quay. In the 18th and 19th centuries Clovelly had a large fishing fleet which flourished in the herring trade. In the 1820s there were so many boats working out of Clovelly that the quay had to be lengthened to accommodate them all.

East of Clovelly along the coast path is the peaceful little hamlet of **Buck's Mills** (*right*). Here a single narrow street lined with cottages runs down to the sea where rock pools are revealed on the small sand and pebble beach at low tide. At one time limestone was shipped here from South Wales to be processed for use by farmers. On a plateau beneath the cliffs at **Hartland Point** (*bottom*) a lighthouse warns seafarers away from this dangerous, rocky headland. The harbour at Hartland Quay was originally paid for in the 16th century by Sir Francis Drake, Sir Walter Raleigh and Sir John Hawkins to provide a safe refuge on this notoriously treacherous stretch of coast. Once well used by local industry, the quay was almost completely destroyed by storms in the 19th century. The smooth contours of Lundy Island are visible on the horizon some twelve miles away.

A former Augustinian monastery, **Hartland Abbey** (*right*) is set in a narrow, sheltered valley near Bideford. Garden designer Gertrude Jekyll used to be a guest at the abbey and she is thought to be responsible for some of the design, including the Victorian fernery. Built on the sides of the valley to avoid the prevailing winds, a series of walled gardens is stocked with herbaceous plants, roses, clematis and vegetables. In spring and early summer the slopes are clothed by the profusion of azaleas, rhododendrons, camellias, hydrangeas and gunnera. Water is an important feature of the design of the gardens at **Docton Mill** (*below*) which occupies the site of a derelict Saxon water-mill. Here there are many small streams, ponds and leats which provide ideal conditions for water-loving plants. When this garden was created in the 1980s, the intention was to make a natural display integrating cultivated areas with the wild. The result is a magnificent array of traditional spring flowers such as narcissi, bluebells and primulas alongside the more exotic. In summer, the colour and scent of roses, including many old shrub roses, fills the garden.